Leaping Poetry

*An Idea with Poems
and Translations*

SEVENTIES PRESS BOOKS PUBLISHED BY BEACON PRESS

Forty Poems Touching on Recent American History
Edited by Robert Bly

The Sea and the Honeycomb
A Book of Tiny Poems
Edited by Robert Bly

Neruda and Vallejo
Selected Poems
Edited by Robert Bly

Miguel Hernandez and Blas de Otero
Selected Poems
Edited by Timothy Baland and Hardie St. Martin

Lorca and Jiménez
Selected Poems
Chosen and Translated by Robert Bly

Friends, You Drank Some Darkness
Three Swedish Poets
Martinson, Ekelöf, and Tranströmer
Chosen and Translated by Robert Bly

Leaping Poetry
An Idea with Poems and Translations
Robert Bly

Leaping Poetry

An Idea
with Poems
and
Translations

Robert Bly

A SEVENTIES PRESS BOOK

Beacon Press : Boston

Copyright © 1975 by Robert Bly
Copyright © 1972 by The Seventies Press
Beacon Press books are published under the auspices
of the Unitarian Universalist Association
Published simultaneously in hardcover and paperback editions
Simultaneous publication in Canada by Saunders of Toronto, Ltd.
All rights reserved
Printed in the United States of America

9 8 7 6 5 4 3 2 1

Library of Congress Cataloging in Publication Data

Main entry under title:
Leaping poetry.
  "A Seventies Press book."
  English, or English and Spanish.
  1. Poetry, Modern—20th Century. 2. Poetry.
I. Bly, Robert.
PN6099.L4   808.81   73-6243
ISBN 0-8070-6392-4
ISBN 0-8070-6393-2 (pbk.)

So many things fail to interest us, simply because they don't find in us enough surfaces on which to live, and what we have to do then is to increase the number of planes in our mind, so that a much larger number of themes can find a place in it at the same time.

Ortega y Gasset

I am thirsty for odors and laughs,
I am thirsty for new poems,
poems with no lilies or moons,
and no love affairs about to fail.

Garcia Lorca

Contents

Leaping Poetry

*An Idea with Poems
and Translations*

LOOKING FOR DRAGON SMOKE

1.

IN ANCIENT times, in the "time of inspiration", the poet flew from one world to another, "riding on dragons", as the Chinese said. Isaiah rode on those dragons, so did Li Po and Pindar. They dragged behind them long tails of dragon smoke. Some of that dragon smoke still boils out of Beowulf. The Beowulf poet holds tight to Danish soil, or leaps after Grendel into the sea.

This dragon smoke means that a leap has taken place in the poem. In many ancient works of art we notice a long floating leap at the center of the work. That leap can be described as a leap from the conscious to the unconscious and back again, a leap from the known part of the mind to the unknown part and back to the known. In the epic of Gilgamesh, which takes place in a settled society, psychic forces suddenly create Enkidu, "the hairy man", as a companion for Gilgamesh, who is becoming too successful. The reader has to leap back and forth between the white man, "Gilgamesh", and the "hairy man". In the *Odyssey* the travellers visit a Great Mother island, dominated by the Circe-Mother, and are turned into pigs. They make the leap in an instant. In all art derived from Great Mother mysteries, the leap to the unknown part of the mind lies in the very center of the work. The strength of "classical art" has much more to do with this leap than with the order that the poets developed to contain, and, partially, to disguise it.

As Christian civilization took hold, and the power of the spiritual patriarchies deepened, this leap occurred less and less often in Western literature. Obviously the ethical ideas of Christianity inhibit it. From the start Christianity has been against the leap. Christian ethics always embodied a move against the "animal instincts"; Christian thought, especially Paul's thought, builds a firm distinction between spiritual energy and animal energy, a distinction so sharp it became symbolized by black and white. White became associated with the conscious and black with the unconscious. Christianity taught its poets — we are among them — to leap *away* from the unconscious, not *toward* it.

The intellectual Western mind accepted the symbolism of white and black, and far from trying to unite both in a circle, as the Chinese did, tried to get "apartheid". In the process, some weird definitions of words developed.

If a European avoided the animal instincts and consistently leaped away from the unconscious, he was said to be living in a state of "innocence". Children were thought to be "innocent" because it was believed they had no sexual, that is, animal, instincts. Eighteenth century translators like Pope and Dryden forced Greek and Roman literature to be their allies in their leap away from animality, and they translated Homer as if he too were "innocent". To Christian Europeans, impulses open to the sexual instincts or animal instincts indicated a fallen state, a state of "experience".

Blake thought the whole nomenclature insane, the precise reverse of the truth. He wrote *The Songs of Innocence and Experience* about that. In that book he reversed the poles. He maintained that living open to animal instincts was precisely "innocence"; children were innocent exactly because they moved back and forth between the known and unknown minds with a minimum of fear. To write well, you must "become like little children". Blake, discussing "experience", declared that to be afraid of a leap into the unconscious is actually to be in a state of "experience". (We are all experienced in that fear.) The state of "experience" is characterized by blocked love-energy,

2

boredom, envy, and joylessness. Another characteristic is a pedestrian movement of the mind; possibly constant fear makes the mind move slowly. Blake could see that after eighteen hundred years of no-leaping, joy was disappearing, poetry was dying, "the languid strings do scarcely move! The sound is forced, the notes are few." A nurse in the state of "experience", obsessed with a fear of animal blackness (a fear which increased after the whites took Africa), calls the children in from play as soon as the light falls:

> When the voices of children are heard on the green
> And whisp'rings are in the dale,
> The days of my youth rise fresh in my mind,
> My face turns green and pale.
>
> Then come home, my children, the sun is gone down
> And the dews of night arise;
> Your spring and your day are wasted in play
> And your winter and night in disguise.

The nurse in "The Songs of Innocence" also calls the children in. But she is not in a state of "experience", and when the children say:

> "No, no, let us play, for it is yet day
> And we cannot go to sleep;
> Besides in the sky the little birds fly
> And the hills are all cover'd with sheep."

She replies:

> "Well, well, go and play till the light fades away
> And then go home to bed."
> The little ones leaped and shouted and laugh'd
>   And all the hills echoed.

She enjoys their shouts. They leap about on the grass playing, as an "innocent man" leaps about inside his psyche.

My idea, then, is that a great work of art often has at its center a long floating leap, around which the work of art in ancient times used to gather itself like steel shavings around the magnet. But a work of art does not necessarily have at its center a single long floating leap. The work can have many leaps, perhaps shorter. The real joy of poetry is to experience this leaping inside a poem. A poet who is "leaping" makes a jump from an object soaked in unconscious substance to an object or idea soaked in conscious psychic substance. What is marvellous is to see this leaping return in poetry of this century.

So far the leaps tend to be fairly short. In "Nothing But Death" Neruda leaps from death to the whiteness of flour, then to notary publics, and he continues to make leap after leap. We often feel elation reading Neruda because he follows some arc of association which corresponds to the inner life of the objects; so that anyone sensitive to the inner life of objects can ride with him. The links are not private, but somehow bound into nature.

Thought of in terms of language, then, leaping is the ability to associate fast. In a great ancient or modern poem, the considerable distance between the associations, the distance the spark has to leap, gives the lines their bottomless feeling, their space, and the speed of the association increases the excitement of the poetry.

2.

Sometime in the thirteenth century poetry in Europe began to show a distinct decline in the ability to associate powerfully. There are individual exceptions, but the circle of worlds pulled into the poem by association dwindles after Chaucer and Langland; their work is already a decline from the Beowulf-poet. By the eighteenth century, the dwindling had become a psychic disaster. Freedom of association had become drastically curtailed. The word "sylvan" by some psychic railway line leads directly to "nymph", to "lawns", to "dancing", so to "reason", to music, spheres, heavenly order, etc. They're all stops on some railroad. There are very few images of the Snake, or the Dragon, or the Great Mother, and if mention is made, the Great Mother leads to no other images, but rather to words suggesting paralysis or death. As Pope said, "The proper study of mankind is man."

The loss of associative freedom showed itself in form as well as in content. In content the poet's thought plodded through the poem, line after line, like a man being escorted through a prison. The "form" was a corridor, full of opening and closing doors. The rhymed lines opened at just the right moment, and closed again behind the visitors.

By the eighteenth century the European intellectual was no longer interested in imagination really. He was trying to develop the "masculine" mental powers he sensed Socrates stood for — a de-mythologized intelligence, that moves in a straight line made of tiny bright links, an intelligence dominated by linked facts rather than "irrational" feelings. The European intellectual succeeded in developing that rationalist intelligence and it was to prove useful. Industry needed it to guide a locomotive through a huge freight yard, or to guide a spaceship back from the moon through the "re-entry corridor".

Nevertheless, this careful routing of psychic energy, first done in obedience to Christian ethics, and later in obedience to commercial needs, had a crippling effect upon the psychic life. The process amounted to an inhibiting of psychic flight, and as Blake saw, once the child had finished European schools, he was incapable of flight. He lived the rest of his life with "single vision and Newton's sleep".

Blake took the first step: he abducted the thought of poetry and took it off to some obscure psychic woods. Those woods were real woods, occult ceremonies took place in them, as they had in ancient woods. In Germany, Novalis and Hölderlin abducted a child, also, and raised it deep in the forest. All over Europe energy in poetry began to come more and more from the unconscious, from the black side of the intelligence. Freud pointed out that the dream still retained the fantastic freedom of association known to us before only from ancient art. By the end of the nineteenth century, both the poem and the dream had been set free: they were no longer part of the effort to develop Socratic intelligence. The poets then began to devote their lives to deepening the range of association in the poem, and increasing the speed of association.

It is this movement that has given such fantastic energy and excitement to "modern poetry" in all European countries. The movement has been partly successful; after only a hundred years of effort, some of the psychic ability to fly has been restored. I will concentrate here on leaping poetry, and try to give some examples of it.

Robert Bly

FEDERICO GARCIA LORCA

LANDSCAPE WITH TWO GRAVES
AND AN ASSYRIAN HOUND

Friend,
get up so you can hear the Assyrian
hound howling.
The three nymphs of cancer are up and dancing,
my son.
They brought along mountains of red sealing-wax
and some rough sheets that cancer slept on last night.
The neck of the horse had an eye
and the moon was up in a sky so cold
she had to rip up her own mound of Venus
and drown the ancient cemeteries in blood and ashes.

Friend,
wake up, for the hills are still not breathing,
and the grass in my heart has gone off somewhere.
It does not matter if you are full of sea-water.
I loved a child for a long time
who had a tiny feather on his tongue
and we lived a hundred years inside a knife.
Wake up. Say nothing. Listen. Sit up a little.
The howling
is a long and purple tongue leaving behind
ants of terror and lilies that make you drunk.
It's coming now near your stone. Don't stretch out your
        roots!
Nearer. It's moaning. Do not cry in your sleep, my friend.

My friend, get up
so you can hear the Assyrian
hound howling.

Translated by Robert Bly

7

PEQUEÑO POEMA INFINITO

Equivocar el camino
es llegar a la nieve
y llegar a la nieve
es pacer durante veinte siglos las hierbas de los
        cementerios.

Equivocar el camino
es llegar a la mujer,
la mujer que no teme la luz,
la mujer que mata dos gallos en un segundo,
la luz que no teme a los gallos
y los gallos que no saben cantar sobre la nieve.

Pero si la nieve se equivoca de corazón
puede llegar el viento Austro
y como el aire no hace caso de los gemidos
tendremos que pacer otra vez las hierbas de los
        cementerios.
Yo vi dos dolorosas espigas de cera
que enterraban un paisaje de volcanes
y vi dos niños locos que empujaban llorando las pupilas
        de un asesino.

Pero el dos no ha sido nunca un número
porque es una angustia y su sombra
porque es la guitarra donde el amor se desespera,
porque es la demostración de otro infinito que no es suyo

LITTLE INFINITE POEM

To take the wrong road
is to arrive at the snow
and to arrive at the snow
is to get down on all fours for twenty centuries and eat
       the grasses of the cemeteries.

To take the wrong road
is to arrive at woman,
woman who isn't afraid of light,
woman who kills two roosters in one second,
light which isn't afraid of roosters,
and roosters who don't know how to sing on top of the
       snow.

But if the snow took the wrong heart
the southern wind could very well arrive,
and since the air cares nothing for groans
we will have to get down on all fours again and eat the
       grasses of the cemeteries.

I saw two mournful wheat heads made of wax
burying a countryside of volcanoes;
and I saw two insane little boys who wept as they leaned
       on a murderer's eyeballs.

But two, that is not a number!
All it is is an agony and its shadow,
it's only the guitar where love feels its discouragement,
it's only the demonstration of something else's infinity,

y es las murallas del muerto
y el castigo de la nueva resurrección sin finales.

Los muertos odian el número dos
pero el número dos adormece a las mujeres
y como la mujer teme la luz
la luz tiembla delante de los gallos
y los gallos sólo saben volar sobre la nieve
tendremos que pacer sin descanso las hierbas de los
    cementerios.

a castle raised around a dead man,
and the scourging of the new resurrection that will never
    end.

Dead people hate the number two,
but the number two makes women drop off to sleep,
and since women are afraid of light
light shudders when it has to face the roosters,
and since all roosters know is how to fly over the snow
we will have to get down on all fours and eat the grasses
    of the cemeteries forever.

Translated by Robert Bly

CHU YUAN

THE HOLY ONE OF THE RIVER

We two are exploring the Nine Rivers together.
Storm winds fall, sweeping up the water.
I ride in the water-car, its roof is all lily pads,
a naked-headed snake and two dragons are pulling it.
From K'un-lung Mountain I can see in all directions.
My spirit goes walking around on the face of the deep.
Getting dark. But I'm confused and forget home.
I daydream of some shore a long way off.
Tell me, spirit, why do you live in a mansion
made of fish-scales, in a hall inhabited by dragons,
its portico made of sea-shells, a mother-of-pearl tower?
Why do you go on living here in the water?
I ride the white tortoise, you take me all through
the tiny islands, we scoot after speckled fish.
The rapid water plunges downstream.
You turn to the east and make a gentle bow.
I see the one I love safely to south harbor.
Wave after wave comes and urges me to come in.
Thousands of fishes tell me goodbye!

Translated by Ho Yen Chi

SHINKICHI TAKAHASHI

FISH

I hold a newspaper, reading.
Suddenly my hands become cow ears,
They turn into Pusan, the South Korean port.

Lying on a mat
Spread on the bankside stones,
I fell asleep.
But a willow leaf, breeze-stirred,
Brushed my ear.
I remained just as I was,
Near the murmurous water.

When young there was a girl
Who became a fish for me.
Whenever I wanted fish
Broiled in salt, I'd summon her.
She'd get down on her stomach
To be sun-cooked on the stones.
And she was always ready!

Alas, she no longer comes to me.
And old benighted drake,
I hobble homeward.
But look, my drake feet become horse hoofs!
Now they drop off
And, stretching marvellously
Become the tracks of the Tokaido Railway Line.

Translated by Lucien Stryk

SPANISH LEAPING

IT'S ODD how seldom American poets or critics mention association when they talk of poetry. A good leap is thought of as a lucky strike if it appears in the poem, wonderful; if not, no one thinks the worse of it. The leaps in a man like Patchen are never talked of; instead people think of him as an angry poet or a social poet. The absence of association leads to no conclusion either. We accept tons of dull poetry, and no one looks for an explanation of why it is dull. We are not *aware* of association. The content of a poem is thought to be important, and rapid association is a "device" or "technique" (as A.M. Rosenthal calls it), which can be applied or not, depending on what school you belong to!

But it is possible that rapid association is a form of content. For example, a poem on the Vietnam war with swift association and a poem with dull association have two different contents, perhaps even two different subject matters.

The early poems of Wallace Stevens are some of the few poems in English in which it is clear that the poet himself considered association to be a form of content. Often in *Harmonium*, his first book, the *content* of the poem lies in the *distance* between what Stevens was given as fact, and what he then imagined. The farther a poem gets from its initial worldly circumstance without breaking the thread, the more content it has. In "The Emperor of Ice Cream", for example, the chances are he is watching a child put together a funeral for her doll. That is the worldly fact. He begins to associate:

> Take from the dresses of deal,
> Lacking the three glass knobs, that sheet

14

> *On which she embroidered fantails once*
> *And spread it so as to cover her face.*
> *If her horny feet protrude, they come*
> *To show how cold she is, and dumb.*
> *Let the lamp affix its beam.*
> *The only emperor is the emperor of ice-cream.*

That's a wonderful leap there. Yet the odd thing is that if he had described the play funeral directly, that is, with dull association, the poem would have had no content. As "On the Manner of Addressing Clouds" begins, I suspect he is watching a Yale commencement. This comes out:

> *Gloomy grammarians in golden gowns,*
> *meekly you keep the mortal rendezvous,*
> *eliciting the still sustaining pomps*
> *of speech which are like music so profound,*
> *they seem an exaltation without sound.*

At the end, he suggests that the "pomps of speech" are important, if the grammarians in the drifting waste of the world are to be accompanied by more than "mute bare splendors of the sun and moon."

About the old banal American realism *á la* Bret Harte, he says:

> *Ach, Mutter,*
> *this old black dress,*
> *I have been embroidering*
> *French flowers on it.*

The flowers are French because the French poets were the first, as a group, to adopt underground passages of association as the major interest. We hide all that by calling them symbolists, but poet after poet through several generations gave his entire work to exploring these paths of association — Gérard de Nerval, Lautréamont, Aloysius Bertrand, Baudelaire, Mallarmé, also Poulet, whom Wallace Stevens, in some *Harmonium* poems, resembles fantastically. Eliot too entered association through a French poet.

But the Spanish poets of this century — much greater

than the French in my opinion — loved the new paths of association even more than the French. They considered them *roads*. Antonio Machado says:

> Why should we call
> these accidental furrows roads? . . .
> Everyone who moves on walks
> like Jesus, on the sea.

Machado noticed that fear of sinking prevents many men from association, or "walking":

> Mankind owns four things
> that are no good at sea.
> Anchor, rudder, oars,
> and the fear of going down.

Machado says:

> It doesn't matter now if the golden wine
> overflows from your crystal goblet,
> or if the sour wine dirties the pure glass . . .

> You know the secret corridors
> of the soul, the roads that dreams take,
> and the calm evening
> where they go to die . . . .

Machado's calmness comes from the fact that he *does* know the secret roads. He has positively abandoned the old poetry, which we described as following association railways. Much of the hysteria of contemporary American poetry, especially of the 40's poets, comes from the poet's intense longing to use the old railroads of association; but when he does so he finds they didn't lead anywhere. This is the hysteria that underlies Lowell's *Notebooks*.

Machado abandoned them. He is calm because he *knows* that something new has happened to the western mind, at least it happened to his! (he can't tell if it only happened to him or also to many others). In any case the change makes him joyful:

While dreaming, perhaps, the hand
of the man who broadcasts the stars like grain
made the lost music start once more
like the note from a huge harp,
and the frail wave came to our lips
in the form of one or two words that had some truth.

Juan Ramon Jiménez, who made marvellous gifts to
the opening of wider association, has a powerful image for
the discovery of new associative depths to the mind:

OCEANS

I have a feeling that my boat
has struck, down there in the depths,
against a great thing.

And nothing
happens! Nothing . . . Silence . . . Waves . . .

Nothing happens! Or has everything happened,
and are we standing now, quietly, in the new life?

The "new" at the end could be the new life, or the new
association, or the new depth, or the new spirituality —
in Spanish he refuses to be specific. In a late poem called
"Dawn Outside the City Walls" he makes an interesting
distinction between true joy and false joy:

You can see the face of everything, and it is white —
plaster, nightmare, adobe, anemia, cold —
turned to the east. Oh closeness to life!
Hardness of Life! Like something
in the body that is animal — root, slag-ends —
with the soul still not set well there —
and mineral and vegetable!
Sun standing stiffly against man,
against the sow, the cabbages, the mud wall!
— False joy, because you are merely
in time, as they say, and not in the soul!

So much of the experience of the ecstatic widening of
association has been denied to us, because poetry in Spanish is still underrated and underread. The American poets
of the 40's and 50's did not read the Spanish poets. The

poets didn't read them, and so they didn't translate them. Instead translations were done by professors and scholars. When these men and women, with good will on the whole, translated the leaping Spanish poets, they changed the great Spanish leaps back into the short plodding steps we were used to, they translated wild association into dull association. The translators of Rilke — Leishman, the worst — did the same thing. It's wrong to blame them — they couldn't do anything else, but the reason they are not poets is precisely because they can only take the leaps that have already been taken many times before. The only way out then is for the American poets themselves to translate the Spaniards.

A second thing that has kept us from being aware of association as the core of a poem is the grudge American critics and university teachers have always had against surrealism. Philip Lamantia, Robert Duncan and others write of, and to some extent, out of, Breton surrealism, and regarded French surrealism as far superior to other sorts; but all through the fifties and sixties we didn't have a single important surrealist magazine in the United States. A small magazine has recently been started in San Francisco, *Anti-Narcissus*, which is devoted to French surrealism and it is good. We still don't have a magazine to represent Spanish surrealism, to say nothing of German, or Greek.

American poetry faltered in the 40's and 50's: we can make a generalization: if the Americans do not have European poets to refresh their sense of what association is, their work soon falls back to the boring associative tracks that so many followed through the *Kenyon Review* times and the dull political landscapes of the *Partisan Review*.

The American poets are now turning to Lorca, Vallejo and Neruda for help. Lorca and the South Americans learned swift associations from Quevedo, Goya, Becquer, Juan Ramon. Vallejo especially is a genius in association.

Eshleman worked hard, but he lacks all sense of joy, and his Vallejo translations once more transform ecstatic leaps back into dull association. So I have included here a few newly translated poems of Vallejo, from *Poemas Humanos*, to indicate his swiftness. Neruda doesn't move as fast, but he puts his feet down with great firmness.

Robert Bly

SHINKICHI TAKAHASHI

POTATO

Inside of one potato
there are mountains and rivers.

Translated by Harold P. Wright

POEMA PARA SER LEIDO Y CANTADO

Sé que hay una persona
que me busca en su mano, día y noche,
encontrandome, a cada minuto, en su calzado.
¿Ignora que la noche está enterrada
con espuelas detrás de la cocina?

Sé que hay una persona compuesta de mis partes,
a la que integro cuando va mi talle
cabalgando en su exacta piedrecilla.
¿Ignora que a su cofre
no volverá moneda que salió con su retrato?

Sé el día,
pero el sol se me ha escapado;
sé el acto universal que hizo en su cama
con ajeno valor y esa agua tibia, cuya
superficial frecuencia es una mina.
¿Tan pequeña es, acaso, esa persona,
que hasta sus proprios pies así la pisan?

Un gato es el lindero entre ella y yo,
al lado mismo de su taza de agua.
La veo en las esquinas, se abre y cierra
su veste, antes palmera interrogante . . .
¿Qué podrá hacer sino cambiar de llanto?

Pero me busca y busca. ¡Es una historia!

POEM TO BE READ AND SUNG

I know there is someone
looking for me day and night inside her hand,
and coming upon me, each moment, in her shoes.
Doesn't she know the night is buried
with spurs behind the kitchen?

I know there is someone composed of my pieces,
whom I complete when my waist
goes galloping on her precise little stone.
Doesn't she know that money spent for her likeness
never returns to her trunk?

I know the day,
but the sun has escaped from me;
I know the universal act she performed in her bed
with some other woman's bravery and warm water, whose
shallow recurrence is a mine.
Is it possible this being is so small
even her own feet walk on her that way?

A cat is the border between us two,
right there beside her bowl of water.
I see her on the corners, her dress — once
an inquiring palm tree — opens and closes . . . .
What can she do but change her style of weeping?

But she does look and look for me. This is a true story!

Translated by James Wright and Robert Bly

CESAR VALLEJO

TENGO UN MIEDO TERRIBLE...

Tengo un miedo terrible de ser un animal
de blanca nieve, que sostuvo padre
y madra, con su sola circulación venosa,
y que, esto día espléndido, solar y arzobispal,
día que representa así a la noche,
linealmente
elude este animal estar contento, respirar
y transformarse y tener plata.

Sería pena grande
que fuera yo tan hombre hasta ese punto.
Un disparate, una premisa ubérrima
a cuyo yugo ocasional sucumbe
el gonce espiritual de mi cintura.
Un disparate ... En tanto,
es así, más acá de la cabeza de Dios,
en la tabla de Locke, de Bacon, en el lívido pescuezo
de la bestia, en el hocico del alma.

Y, en lógica aromática,
tengo ese mido práctico, este día
espléndido, lunar, de ser aquél, éste talvez,
a cuyo olfato huele a muerto el suelo,
el disparate vivo y el disparate muerto.

¡Oh revolcarse, estar, toser, fajarse,
fajarse la doctrina, la sien, de un hombre al otro,
alajarse, llorar, darlo por ocho
o por siete o por seis, por cinco o darlo
por la vida que tiene tres potencias!

I HAVE A TERRIBLE FEAR...

I have a terrible fear that I may be an animal
of white snow, who has kept his father and mother
alive with his solitary circulation through the veins,
and a fear that on this day which is so marvellous, sunny,
       archbishoprical,
(a day that stands so for night)
this animal, like a straight line,
will manage not to be happy, or to breathe,
or to turn into something else, or to get money.

It would be a terrible thing
if I were a lot of man up to that point.
Unthinkable nonsense . . . . an over-fertile assumption
to whose accidental yoke the spiritual
hinge in my waist succumbs.
Unthinkable . . . . Meanwhile
that's how it is on this side of God's head,
in the tabula of Locke, and of Bacon, in the pale neck
of the beast, in the snout of the soul.

And, in fragrant logic,
I do have that practical fear, this marvellous
moony day of being that one, this one maybe,
to whose nose the ground smells like a corpse,
the unthinkable alive and the unthinkable dead.

Oh to roll on the ground, to be there, to cough,
       to wrap oneself,
to wrap the doctrine, the temple, from shoulder to
       shoulder,
to go away, to cry, to let it go for eight
or for seven or for six, for five, or let it go
for life with its three possibilities!

Translated by Robert Bly

THE RUINED STREET

A tongue from different eras of time is moving
over the injured iron, over the eyes
of plaster. It's a tail of harsh
horsehair, stone hands stuffed with rage,
and the house colors fall silent, and the decisions
of the architecture explode,
a ghastly foot makes the balconies filthy,
so slowly, with saved-up shadow,
with face masks bitten by winter and leisure,
the days with their high foreheads drift between
the houses with no moon.

The water and the customs and the white mud
that the star sprinkles down and especially
the air that the bells have beaten in their rage
are wearing things out, they brush
the wheels, pause
at the cigar shops,
and red hair grows on the cornices
like a long sorrow, while keys are falling
into the hole, watches,
and flowers adjusted to nothingness.

Where is the newly born violet? Where are
the necktie and the virginal red yarn?
A tongue of rotten dust is moving forward
over the cities
smashing rings, eating away the paint,
making the black chairs howl soundlessly,
burying the cement florals, the parapets
of mangled metal,

the orchard and the wool, the fiery and blown-up
    photographs
injured by the rain, the thirst of the bedrooms,
    and the huge
movie posters in which the panther
is wrestling with thunder,
the geranium-spears, granaries full of lost honey,
the cough, the suits with their metallic threads,
everything gets covered with a deathly flavor
of regression and dampness and damage.

It's possible that the conversations now underway,
    the bodies brushing,
the chastity of the tired ladies who make their nest in the
    smoke,
the tomatoes murdered without mercy,
the horses of a depressed regiment going by,
the light, the pressure of nameless fingertips,
are wearing out the flat fiber of the lime,
surrounding the building fronts with neuter air
like knives: while
the dangerous air goes chewing up the way we stay alive,
the bricks, the salt runs over like waters,
and the carts with fat axles go bumping by.

Surf of broken roses and tiny holes! Future
of the perfumed vein! Merciless objects!
Do not move, anyone! Do not open your arms
while in the blind water!
Oh motion, oh name that is gravely wounded,
oh spoonful of bewildered wind,
and knocked-around color! Oh wound into which
the blue guitars fall and are killed!

Translated by Robert Bly

25

¡Y SI DESPUES DE TANTAS PALABRAS...

¡Y si después de tantas palabras,
no sobrevive la palabra!
¡Si después de las alas de los pájaros,
no sobrevive el pájara parado!
¡Más valdría, en verdad,
que se lo coman todo y acabemos!

¡Haber nacido para vivir de nuestra muerte!
¡Levantarse del cielo hacia la tierra
por susproprios desastres
y espiar el momento de apagar con su sombra su tiniebla!
¡Más valdría, francamente,
que se lo coman todo y qué más da! . . .

¡Y si después de tanta historia, sucumbimos,
no ya de eternidad,
sino de esas cosas sencillas, como estar
en le casa o ponerse a cavilar!
¡Y si luego encontramos,
de buenas a primeras, que vivimos,
a juzgar por la altura de los astros,
por el peine y las manchas del pañuelo!
¡Más valdría, en verdad,
que se lo coman todo, desde luego!

Se dirá que tenemos
en uno de los ojos mucha pena
y también en el otro, mucha pena
y en los dos, cuando miran, mucha pena . . .
¡Entonces! . . . ¡Claro! . . . Entonces . . . ¡ni palabra!

CESAR VALLEJO

AND WHAT IF AFTER SO MANY WORDS...

And what if after so many words,
the word itself doesn't survive!
And what if after so many wings of birds
the stopped bird doesn't survive!
It would be better then, really,
if it were all swallowed up, and let's end it!

To have been born only to live off our own death!
To raise ourselves from the heavens toward the earth
carried up by our own bad luck,
always watching for the moment to put out our darkness
        with our shadow!
It would be better, frankly,
if it were all swallowed up, and the hell with it!

And what if after so much history, we succumb,
not to eternity,
but to these simple things, like being
at home, or starting to brood!
What if we discover later
all of a sudden, that we are living
to judge by the height of the stars
off a comb and off stains on a handkerchief!
It would be better, really,
if it were all swallowed up, right now!

They'll say that we have a lot
of grief in one eye, and a lot of grief
in the other also, and when they look
a lot of grief in both . . . .
Well then! . . . .Wonderful! . . .Then . . . Don't say a word!

Translated by Douglas Lawder and Robert Bly

WILD ASSOCIATION

ONE DISTINCTION between Spanish surrealism and French surrealism is that the Spanish "surrealist" or "leaping" poet often enters into his poem with a heavy body of feeling piled up behind him as if behind a dam. As you begin the Spanish poem, a heavy river rolls over you. Vallejo's poem "What if after so many words . . ." is a good example of this. And what an incredible poem it is!

French surrealism and Spanish surrealism both contain wonderful leaps, but whereas French surrealism often longs for the leaps *without* any specific emotion — many believe that the unconscious does not *have* emotions — the Spanish poets believe that it does. The poet enters the poem excited, with the emotions alive; he is angry or ecstatic, or disgusted. There are a lot of exclamation marks, visible or invisible. Almost all the poems in Lorca's *Poet in New York* are written with the poet profoundly moved, flying. Powerful feeling makes the mind associate faster, and evidently the presence of swift association makes the emotions still more alive; it increases the adrenalin flow, just as chanting awakens many emotions that the chanter was hardly aware of at the moment he began chanting.

When the poet brings to the poem emotions from his thought-life and his flight-life, emotions which would be intense whether the poem were written or not, and when he succeeds in uniting them with the associative powers of the unconscious, we have something different from Homer or Machado; a new kind of poem (apparently very rare in the nineteenth century) which we could call the poem of "passionate association", or "poetry of flying".

Lorca wrote a beautiful and great essay called "Theory and Function of the Duende", available in English in the

Penguin Lorca. "Duende" is the sense of the presence of death, and Lorca says:

> Very often intellect is poetry's enemy because it is too much given to imitation, because it lifts the poet to a throne of sharp edges and makes him oblivious of the fact that he may suddenly be devoured by ants, or a great arsenic lobster may fall on his head.

Duende involves a kind of elation when death is present in the room, it is associated with "dark" sounds, and when a poet has duende inside him, he brushes past death with each step, and in that presence associates fast (Samuel Johnson remarked that there was nothing like a sentence of death in half an hour to wonderfully clear the mind). The gypsy flamenco dancer is associating fast when she dances, and so is Bach writing his Cantatas. Lorca mentions an old gypsy dancer who, on hearing Brailowsky play Bach, cried out, "That has duende!"

Lorca says:

> To help us seek the duende there are neither maps nor discipline. All one knows is that it burns the blood like powdered glass, that it exhausts, that it rejects all the sweet geometry one has learned, that it breaks with all styles ... that it dresses the delicate body of Rimbaud in an acrobat's green suit: or that it puts the eyes of a dead fish on Count Lautréamont in the early morning Boulevard.

> The magical quality of a poem consists in its being always possessed by the duende, so that whoever beholds it is baptized with dark water.

What is the opposite of wild association then? Tame association? Approved association? Sluggish association? Whatever we want to call it, we know what it is — that slow plodding association that pesters us in so many poetry magazines, and in our own work when it is no good, association that takes half an hour to compare a childhood accident to a crucifixion, or a leaf to the I Ching. Poetry is killed for students in high school by teachers who only understand this dull kind of association, while their students are associating faster and faster.

The Protestant embarrassment in the presence of death turns us into muse poets or angel poets, associating timidly. Lorca says:

> *The duende — where is the duende? Through the empty arch comes an air of the mind that blows insistently over the heads of the dead, in search of the new landscapes and unsuspected accents; an air smelling of child's saliva, of pounded grass, and medusal veil announcing the constant baptism of newly created things.*

Robert Bly

LOYALTY

I believe in the human being. I have seen
shoulder bones splintered by bullwhips,
blind souls staggering forward by fits and starts,
(Spanish men on horses
of suffering and of hunger). And I believe it.

I believe in peace. I have seen
high stars, circles of dawn
burst into flame, deep rivers
on fire, human flow
toward another light: I have seen it and I believe it.

I believe in you, my country. I will tell you
what I have seen: lightning flashes
of rage, love in coldness, and a knife
that is yelling, tearing up bits
of bread; still there is darkness standing alone today; I
      have seen it and I believe it.

Translated by Robert Bly

IGLESIA ABANDONADA

(Balada de la Gran Guerra)

Yo tenía un hijo que se llamaba Juan.
Yo tenía un hijo.
Se perdió por los arcos un viernes de todos los muertos.
Lo vi jugar en las últimas escaleras de la misa
y echaba un cubito de hojalata en el corazón del sacerdote.
He golpeado los ataúdes. ¡Mi hijo! ¡Mi hijo! ¡Mi hijo!
Saqué una pata de gallina por detrás de la luna y luego
comprendí que mi niña era un pez
por donde se alejan las carretas.
Yo tenía una niña.
Yo tenía un pez muerto bajo la ceniza de los incensarios.
Yo tenía un mar. ¿De que? ¡Dios mio! ¡Un mar!
Subí a tocar las campanas, pero las frutas tenían gusanos
y las cerrillas apagadas
se comían los trigos de la primavera.
Yo vi la transparente cigüeña de alcohol
mondar las negras cabezas de los soldados agonizantes
y vi las cabañas de goma
donde giraban las copas llenas de lágrimas.
En las anémonas del ofertorio te encontraré, ¡corazón mio!
cuando el sacerdote levante la mula y el buey con sus
        fuertes brazos
para espantar los sapos nocturnos que rondan los helados
        paisajes del cáliz.
Yo tenía un hijo que era un gigante,
pero los muertos son más fuertes y saben devorar pedazos
        de cielo.
Si mi niño hubiera sido un oso,

RUNDOWN CHURCH

(Ballad of the First World War)

I had a son and his name was John.
I had a son.
He disappeared into the vaulted darkness one Friday
    of All Souls.
I saw him playing on the highest steps of the Mass
throwing a little tin pail at the heart of the priest.
I knocked on the coffins. My son! My son! My son!
I drew out a chicken foot from behind the moon and then
I understood that my daughter was a fish
down which the carts vanish.
I had a daughter.
I had a fish dead under the ashes of the incense burner.
I had an ocean. Of what? Good Lord! An ocean!
I went up to ring the bells but the fruit was all wormy
and the blackened match-ends
were eating the spring wheat.
I saw the stork of alcohol you could see through
shaving the black heads of the dying soldiers
and I saw the rubber booths
where the goblets full of tears were whirling.
In the anemones of the offertory I will find you, my love!
when the priest with his strong arms raises up the mule
        and the ox
to scare the nighttime toads that roam in the icy landscapes
        of the chalice.
I had a son who was a giant,
but the dead are stronger and know how to gobble down
        pieces of the sky.
If my son had only been a bear,

yo no temería el sigilo de los caimanes,
ni hubiese visto al mar amarrado a los árboles
para ser fornicado y herido por el tropel de los regimientos.
¡Si mi niño hubiera sido un oso!
Me envolveré sobre esta lona dura para no sentir el frío
      de los musgos.
Sé muy bien que me darán una manga o la corbata;
pero en el centro de la misa yo romperé el timon y entonces
vendrá a la piedra la locura de pingüinos y gaviotas
que harán decir a los que duermen y a los que cantan
      por las esquinas:
él tenía un hijo.
¡Un hijo! ¡Un hijo! Un hijo
que no era mas que suyo, porque era su hijo!
¡Su hijo! ¡Su hijo! ¡Su hijo!

I wouldn't fear the secrecy of the crocodiles
and I wouldn't have seen the ocean roped to the trees
to be raped and wounded by the mobs from the regiment.
If my son had only been a bear!
I'll roll myself in this rough canvas so as not to feel
        the chill of the mosses.
I know very well they will give me a sleeve or a necktie,
but in the innermost part of the Mass I'll smash the rudder
        and then
the insanity of the penguins and seagulls will come to the
        rock
and will make the people sleeping and the people singing
        on the street-corners say:
he had a son.
A son! A son! A son
and it was no one else's, because it was his son!
His son! His son! His son!

Translated by Robert Bly

FEDERICO GARCIA LORCA

NEW YORK

(Officina y Denuncia)

Debajo de las multiplicaciones
hay una gota de sangre de pato.
Debajo de las divisiones
hay una gota de sangre de marinero.
Debajo de las sumas, un rio de sangre tierna;
un rio que viene cantando
por los dormitorios de los arrabales,
y es plata, cemento o brisa
en el alba mentida de New York.
Existen las montañas, lo sé.
Y los anteojos para la sabiduría,
lo sé. Pero yo no he venido a ver el cielo.
He venido para ver la turbia sangre,
la sangre que lleva las máquinas a las cataratas
y el espíritu a la lengua de la cobra.
Todos los días se matan en New York
cuatro millones de patos,
cinco millones de cerdos,
dos mil palomas para el gusto de los agonizantes,
un millón de vacas,
un millón de corderos
y dos millones de gallos
que dejan los cielos hechos añicos.
Más vale sollozar afilando le navaja
o asesinar a los perros en las alucinantes cacerías
que resistir en la madrugada
los interminables trenes de leche,
los interminables trenes de sangre,
y los trenes de rosas maniatadas

NEW YORK

(Office and Attack)

Beneath all the statistics
there is a drop of a duck's blood.
Beneath all the columns
there is a drop of a sailor's blood.
Beneath all the totals, a river of warm blood;
a river that goes singing
past the bedrooms of the suburbs,
and the river is silver, cement, or wind
in the lying daybreak of New York.
The mountains exist, I know that.
And the lenses ground for wisdom,
I know that. But I have not come to see the sky.
I have come to see the stormy blood,
the blood that sweeps the machines to the waterfalls,
and the spirit on to the cobra's tongue.
Every day they kill in New York
ducks, four million,
pigs, five million,
pigeons, two thousand, for the enjoyment of dying men,
cows, one million,
lambs, one million,
roosters, two million,
who turn the sky to small splinters.
You may as well sob filing a razor blade
or assassinate dogs in the hallucinated foxhunts,
as to try to stop in the dawnlight
the endless trains carrying milk,
the endless trains carrying blood,
and the trains carrying roses in chains

por los comerciantes de perfumes.
Los patos y las palomas
y los cerdos y los corderos
ponen sus gotas de sangre
debajo de las multiplicaciones;
y los terribles alaridos de las vacas estrujadas
llenan de dolor el valle
donde el Hudson se emborracha con aceite.
Yo denuncio a toda la gente
que ignora la otra mitad,
la mitad irredimible
que levanta sus montes de cemento
donde laten los corazones
de los animalitos que se olvidan
y donde caeremos todos
en la última fiesta de los taladros.
Os escupo en la cara.
La otra mitad me escucha
devorando, orinando, volando en su pureza
como los niños de las porterías
que llevan frágiles palitos
a los huecos donde se oxidan
las antenas de los insectos.
No es el infierno, es la calle.
No es la muerte, es la tienda de frutas.
Hay un mundo de ríos quebrados y distancias inasibles
en la patita de ese gato quebrada por el automóvil,
y yo oigo el canto de la lombriz
en el corazón de muchas niñas.
Óxido, fermento, tierra estremecida.
Tierra tú mismo que nadas por los números de la oficina.
¿Qué voy a hacer, ordena los paisajes?
¿Ordenar los amores que luego son fotografías,
que luego son pedazos de madera y bocanadas de sangre?

for those in the field of perfume.
The ducks and the pigeons
and the hogs and the lambs
lay their drop of blood down
underneath all the statistics;
and the terrible bawls of the packed-in cattle
fill the valley with suffering
where the Hudson is getting drunk on its oil.
I attack all those persons
who know nothing of the other half,
the half who cannot be saved,
who raise their cement mountains
in which the hearts of the small
animals no one thinks of are beating,
and from which we will all fall
during the final holiday of the drills.
I spit in your face.
The other half hears me,
as they go on eating, urinating, flying in their purity
like the children of the janitors
who carry delicate sticks
to the holes where the antennas
of the insects are rusting.
This is not hell, it is a street.
This is not death, it is a fruit-stand.
There is a whole world of crushed rivers and unachievable
        distances
in the paw of a cat crushed by a car,
and I hear the song of the worm
in the heart of so many girls.
Rust, rotting, trembling earth.
And you are earth swimming through the figures of the
        office.
What shall I do, set the landscapes in order?
Set in place the lovers who will afterwards be photographs,
who will be bits of wood and mouthfuls of blood?

No, no: yo denuncio,
yo denuncio la conjura
de estas desiertas oficinas
que no radian las agonías,
que borran los programas de la selva,
y me ofrezco a ser comido por las vacas estrujadas
cuando sus gritos llenan el valle
donde el Hudson se emborracha con aceite.

No, I won't; I attack,
I attack the conspiring
of these empty offices
that will not broadcast the sufferings,
that rub out the plans of the forest,
and I offer myself to be eaten by the packed-in cattle,
when their mooing fills the valley
where the Hudson is getting drunk on its oil.

Translated by Robert Bly

SOMETHING LIKE A

peace has been destroyed and
the sky is a pitiful tent

And what if instead of going to the theatre this evening
    I went off to Viet-Nam.
Who is writing, who is holding my hand? It is not mine.
Nothing is mine. Neither the mask, nor the role.
And what if this evening

                  I went off to Viet-Nam.
Some poor devil drinks a glass of water. He's not in his
    theatre seat. He sits down.
That makes two of us. The North and the Puppets. Maese
    Pedro is the third one's name, the pimp. And what
    if instead of being called Mureta Sagarminaga
I went off and they called me union union
against the glass of water, thirst, free verse and duty.
On June twenty-fifth we had no weapons.
On July twenty-sixth we had no weapons.
Just a soldier. And millions of projects, and men, but we
    lacked arms.
Missiles in one word.
Here I am sitting in the middle of the rubble of Hue.
Halfway into the Democratic Republic and halfway into
    the other same democratic republic (*sic*).
Standing in front of a stone. At attention. Terribly
    unpreoccupied
about invaders, hearing the airplanes descending climbing
    ripping through
the night — like fabric slitting at one pull.
What are you doing up there? Poor devils, come
and see the performance: sit behind the machine gun.

Listen. You're all going to die. Don't shoot, because you're
     going to die any minute now. All of you.
Shoot shoot shoot shoot shoot because you'll die anyhow.

A tiny glimmer and the day, a specific day, Monday
     February eighteenth circles part of the sky. I'll soon
     be seeing your face
literally ground to bits, at the spot where the airplane
     flashed.
     Come all,
shoot shoot shoot shoot, you only have one more man
     to go.

Something like a line of poetry a dog sniffs at in the trash.

Translated by Hardie St. Martin

¿Y BIEN? ¿TE SANA EL METALOIDE PALIDO...

¿Y bien? ¿Te sana el metaloide pálido?
¿Los metaloides incendiarios, cívicos,
inclinados al río atroz del polvo?

Esclavo, es ya la hora circular
en que las dos aurículas se forman
anillos guturales, corredizos, cuaternarios.

Señor esclavo, en la mañana mágica
se ve, por fin,
el busto de tu trémulo ronquido,
vense tus sufrimientos a caballo,
pasa el órgano bueno, el de tres asas,
hojeo, mes por mes, tu monocorde cabellera,
tu suegra llora
haciendo huesecillos de sus dedos,
se inclina tu alma con pasión a verte
y tu sien, un momento, marca el paso.

Y la gallina pone su infinito, uno por uno;
sale la tierra hermosa de las humeantes sílabas,
te retratas de pie junto a tu hermano,
truena el color esucro bajo el lecho
y corren y entrechócanse los pulpos.

Señor esclavo, ¿y bien?
¿Los metaloides obran en tu angustia?

CESAR VALLEJO

AND SO? THE PALE METALLOID HEALS YOU ...

And so? The pale metalloid heals you?
The flammable metalloids, interior,
leaning toward the hideous river of dust?

Slave, it's now the huge round hour
when the two auricles make
guttural rings, slippery, post-Tertiary.

Esquire slave, the bust of your quivery snore
is visible at last
in the enchanted morning,
your suffering is seen on horseback,
the good organ goes by — the one with three ears —,
I leaf month after month through your long one-stringed
        hair,
your mother-in-law sobs
as she makes tiny bones from her fingers,
your soul bends madly over to see you
and for an instant your temple keeps time.

And the hen lays her infinite, one by one,
handsome earth rises from the smoking syllables,
you get photographed standing by your brother,
the shadowy color thunders under the bed,
the octopuses race around and collide.

And so, esquire slave?
Do the metalloids work well with your anguish?

Translated by Robert Bly

POETRY OF STEADY LIGHT

LET'S LOOK a moment at poems that do not leap about inside the psyche. There are two kinds of poets who are non-leapers, entirely different. We've mentioned the dull stuff, where the poet dislikes all parts of his psyche, and moves around so sluggishly you fall asleep before the poem is over.

Another sort of poetry is written by a poet who remains by choice for the time of the poem roughly in one part of the psyche. His poems give off a steady light (his poetry could perhaps be called Poetry of Steady Light). (The leaping poem by contrast gives off a constantly flashing light as it shifts from light psyche to dark psyche, resembling the flashing lights of flying saucers.)

What is an example of a poem of steady light? Surely "Kore" by Robert Creeley:

> As I was walking
>   I came upon
> chance walking
>   the same road upon.
>
> As I sat down
>   by chance to move
> late
>   if and as I might,
>
> light the wood was,
>   light and green,
> and what I saw
>   before I had not seen.
>
> It was a lady
>   accompanied
> by goat men
>   leading her.

> *Her hair held earth.*
> *Her eyes were dark.*
> *A double flute*
> *made her move.*
>
> *"O love,*
> *where are you*
> *leading*
> *me now?"*

One of the reasons that Creeley does this is because his mind leaps so much "during the day" that in a poem he tries to hold it in one place to stop the chaos. The danger of staying in one part of the psyche during a poem is that eventually you may lose touch with the more primitive, outward, sensual, "dark" areas.

This issue concentrates on "leaping" poetry, but I am not saying that it is the only good kind of poetry. Far from it. I like the poetry of steady light very much. Shakespeare's sonnets are often poetry of steady light, as are some Wordsworth poems, and the poems of Robert Francis. It's clear too that one poet can write both kinds if he wants to. Tomas Transtömer, the young Swedish poet, wrote a poem called "In the Open", printed later in this volume, which inhabits three different sections of the brain in turn. Here is a poem of his that remains in one section:

TRACK

> *2 a.m. moonlight. The train has stopped*
> *out in a field. Far off sparks of light from a town,*
> *flickering coldly on the horizon.*
>
> *As when a man goes so deep into his dream*
> *he will never remember that he was there*
> *when he returns again to his room.*
>
> *Or when a person goes so deep into a sickness*
> *that his days all become some flickering sparks, a swarm,*
> *feeble and cold on the horizon.*
>
> *The train is entirely motionless.*
> *2 o'clock: strong moonlight, few stars.*

LEAPING IN NARRATIVE POETRY

One of the reasons that narrative poetry has collapsed is that most poets have not figured out how to get leaping back into narration. T.S. Eliot, brought up on Browning's narratives, understood that they failed because of lack of leaping. He then tried to make leaps in his narratives in

FEDERICO GARCIA LORCA

REYERTA

En la mitad del barranco
las navajas de Albacete,
bellas de sangre contraria,
relucen como los peces.
Una dura luz de naipe
recorta en el agrio verde
caballos enfurecidos
y perfiles de jinetes.
En la copa de un olivo
lloran dos viejas mujeres.
El toro de la reyerta
se sube por las paredes.
Ángeles negros traían
pañuelos y agua de nieve.
Ángeles con grandes alas
de navajas de Albacete.

The Wasteland *by omitting links. It was a help.*

Lorca worked harder at that problem. He did introduce leaping again into narrative poetry, in his book called Romancero Gitano. I've translated "Quarrel" from that book. Lorca is simply retelling in the poem a typical country story of a fight between two gypsies, told often before in ballads. Here is how it comes out. (Albacete is the place where the best knives in Spain were made—gypsies loved to fight with them.)

FEDERICO GARCIA LORCA

THE QUARREL

The Albacete knives, magnificent
with stranger-blood,
flash like fishes
on the gully slope.
Light crisp as a playing
card snips out of bitter
green the profiles of riders
and maddened horses.
Two old women in an olive
tree are sobbing.
The bull of the quarrel
is rising up the walls.
Black angels arrived
with handkerchiefs and snow water.
Angels with immense wings
like Albacete knives.

Juan Antonio el de Montilla
reuda muerto la pendiente,
su cuerpo lleno de lirios
y una granada en las sienes.
Ahora monta cruz de fuego,
carretera de la muerte.

✤

El juez, con guardia civil,
por los olivares viene.
Sangre resbalada gime
muda canción de serpiente.
"Señores guardia civiles:
aquí pasó lo de siempre.
Han muerto cuatro romanos
y cinco cartagineses."

✤

La tarde loca de higueras
y de rumores calientes
cae desmayada en los muslos
heridos de los jinetes.
Y ángeles negros volaban
por el aire del poniente.
Ángeles de largas trenzas
y corazones de aceite.

Juan Antonio from Montilla
rolls dead down the hill,
his body covered with lilies,
a pomegranate on his temples.
He is climbing now on the cross of fire,
the highway of death.

*

The State Police and the judge
come along through the olive grove.
From the earth loosed blood moans
the silent folksong of the snake.
"Well, your honor, you see,
it's the same old business —
four Romans are dead
and five Carthaginians."

*

Dusk that the fig trees and the
hot whispers have made hysterical
faints and falls on the bloody
thighs of the riders,
and black angels went on flying
through the failing light,
angels with long hair,
and hearts of olive-oil.

Translated by Robert Bly

HOPPING

EUROPEAN POETS led and still remain the leaders in poetry of association. They began it in 1780 while our ancestors in the United States were still a few Puritans dressed in black and white, frightened by the black forests west of them. Some European painters made as great leaps as the poets did, perhaps greater. Max Ernst's leaps are oceanic, and full of distance. Perhaps he's better than any modern French poet, though we remember how close the connection in any event was between poets and painters in France, and Lorca's admiring friendship in the thirties with Dali. In America, the painters and poets have had little in common, and that has contributed to the American poets' unawareness of leaping as a principle in art. Poets like Nims or Shapiro simply do not grasp association, and we notice we never think of them in connection with painting at all. Frank O'Hara had a deep interest in painting in general, especially in French painting, and so does John Ashbery. So we have a link of sorts there. Ashbery has real leaping in his work.

The poets who came out of Ashbery, the St. Mark's and Bolinas group, retain his affection for painting, but unfortunately have no more relation to the intense Spanish poetry than Karl Shapiro has. They leap, but without that "head of emotion" that gives such power to many Spanish works of art. They do not approach the poem with passion at all. That great head of water which Lorca and Vallejo back up over the poem before they set down a word is simply absent (except perhaps in O'Hara's poem for Billie Holiday). O'Hara and Ted Berrigan, to name two extremely talented poets, are both for the most part poets of pleasure, a very different thing from being a poet of emotion.

The St. Mark's poets are very aware of that distinction — this is nothing new to them — and some actually prefer the poetry of pleasure to poetry of intense emotion, and they like the eighteenth century poetry precisely for that reason. Surely in a brutal, job-ridden, Puritanical, Billy Grahamized America, poetry of pleasure, describing the six or seven lovely things you did that day, is a victory of sorts.

The trouble with all that is that the pleasures Berrigan, for instance, describes, tend to be pleasures of the conscious mind and not of the unconscious. Occasionally we find the poets in bed with a woman, but we get little feeling of the mystery of that pleasure. Usually it takes place quickly just before the woman goes off to work. Most of the pleasures both men and women poets describe are of an even more rational sort, like finding the Sunday Times on the doorstep, then throwing it out, or seeing a good movie with Lon Chaney in it, or eating marshmallows in a Chinese restaurant. All of these are what Snyder calls "the pleasures of the educated mind". I think some of Ashbery's poems are great poems, but the generations of these poets clearly make some sort of diminishing tunnel — in each generation the poems of the school get smaller. Tom Clark, Lew Warsh, Anne Waldman, Larry Fagin all suffer from a lack of growth so far — of that group Ted Berrigan and Peter Schjedahl have grow the most — and I think it's partly because this "New York" poetry, though it appears to leap, actually leaps about inside one room of the psyche only. The poems are not flying from the intellect to the sea, from Denmark to the unconscious, they are not going anywhere; in other words, it is not leaping so much as hopping. It's fun to hop — I enjoy watching these poets avoid standing in the same place, keeping their feet in the air. But Max Ernst does a lot more than that.

The St. Mark's poets learned from Creeley to stay in one cave of the mind; but they are not far enough back in that room. There is an agony in Creeley's work, which means he is living far back in the archaic part of his cave. The intensity comes from that, and it is the intensity that makes his best poems give off light. The St. Mark's poets always have a leisure class mood about them; they are essentially the products of a rich country, who see nothing to fight for, and never fight. In a way, they are consumer poets. They refuse to consume cars and steaks, but they consume subtler things — like poetic pleasures.

This is not to say I hate their poetry; on the contrary, I enjoy it, but they long too much to stay in one part of the psyche, a fairly well-lit part, as Hemingway called it, and the result eventually has to be boring. They treat their adopted style as if it were content, but it's only a style. There is nothing sacred about a style. Lorca says duende "rejects all the sweet geometry one has learned, it breaks with all styles . . .".

Here are two Swedish poems with leaping. You'll notice they do not start with the great head of emotion the Spaniards have — but they manage to leap all right.

GUNNAR EKELÖF

MONOLOGUE WITH ITS WIFE

Take two extra-old cabinet ministers and overtake them
    on the North Sea
Provide each of them with a comet in the rear
Seven comets each!
Send a wire:
If the city of Trondheim takes them in it will be bombed
If the suet field allows them to escape it will be bombed
Now you have to signal:
Larger ships approaching
Don't you see, there in the radio! Larger ship
in converging path. Send a warning!
All small strawberry boats shall be ordered to go in to the
    shore and lie down

— Come and help me. I am disappearing.
The god is in the process of transforming me, the one in the
    corner over there (whispering)

Translated by Robert Bly

OUT IN THE OPEN

1.

Late autumn labyrinth.
On the porch of the woods a thrown away bottle.
Go in. Woods are silent abandoned houses this time of year.
Just a few sounds now: as if someone were moving twigs
    around carefully with a pincers
or as if an iron hinge were whining feebly inside a thick
    trunk.
Frost has breathed on the mushrooms and they have
    shrivelled up.
They look like objects and clothing left behind by people
    who've disappeared.
The dusk is coming already. The thing to do now is
    to get out
and find the landmarks again: the rusty machine out
    in the field
and the house on the other side of the lake, a reddish square
    intense as a boullion cube.

2.

A letter from America drove me out again, started me
    walking
through the luminous June night in the empty suburban
    streets
among newborn districts without memories, cool as
    blueprints.

Letter in my pocket. You wild, raging, walking, you are a
    kind of prayer for others.
Over there evil and good actually have faces.
With us for the most part it's a fight between roots,
    numbers, shades of light.

The people who do death's errands don't shy from
    daylight.
They rule from glass offices. They mill about in the bright
    sun.
They lean forward over a table, and throw a look
    to the side.

Far off I found myself standing in front of one of the new
    buildings.
Many windows flowed together there into a single
    window.
The luminous night sky was caught in it, and the walking
    trees.
It was a mirror-like lake with no waves, turned on edge
    in the summer night.

Violence seemed unreal.
for a few moments.

3.

Sun burning. The plane comes in low,
throwing a shadow shaped like a giant cross that rushes
    over the ground.

A man is sitting in the field poking at something.
The shadow arrives.
For a fraction of a second he is right in the center
        of the cross.

I have seen the cross hanging in the cool church vaults.
At times it resembles a split-second shot of something
moving at tremendous speed.

Translated by Robert Bly

THE THREE BRAINS

SOME RECENT brain research throws light I think on what we've been talking about. I'll sum up some of the conclusions and speculations made by the American neurologist, Paul MacLean. I first ran into his ideas in Koestler's book, *The Ghost in the Machine*, where he gives about six pages to MacLean's theories, and refers to the neurological journals in which MacLean publishes. The gist of MacLean's thought is that we do not have one brain, but three. Mac-Lean's map of the head isn't psychological, as Freud's Ego, Id and Superego, but geographical — the three brains are actually in the head, and brain surgeons have known for a long time what they look like. MacLean's contribution has been to suggest that each of these brains is to some extent independent. During evolution, the body often re-shaped the body — fins, for example, in us, turned utterly into arms, but the forward momentum in evolution was apparently so great that the brain could not allow itself the time to reform — it simply added.

The reptile brain is still intact in the head. Known medically as the limbic node, it is a horseshoe shaped organ located in the base of the skull. The job of the reptile brain appears to be the physical survival of the organism in which it finds itself. Should danger or enemies come near, an alarm system comes into play, and the reptile brain takes over from the other brains — it takes what we might call "executive power". In great danger it might hold that power exclusively. It's been noticed, for example, that when mountain climbers are in danger of falling, the brain mood changes — the eyesight intensifies, and the feet "miraculously" take the right steps. Once down the climber realizes he has been "blanked out". This probably means

59

that the reptile brain's need for energy was so great that it withdrew energy even from the memory systems of the mammal and new brains. The presence of fear produces a higher energy input to the reptile brain. The increasing fear in this century means that more and more energy, as a result, is going to the reptile brain: that is the same thing as saying that the military budgets in all nations are increasing.

MacLean himself speculated, in a paper written recently for a philosophical conference, that the persistent trait of paranoia in human beings is due to the inability to shut off the energy source to the reptile brain. In a settled society, if there are no true enemies, the reptile brain will imagine enemies in order to preserve and use its share of the incoming energy. John Foster Dulles represented the reptile brain in the fifties.

When the change to mammal life occurred, a second brain was simply folded around the limbic node. This "cortex", which I will call here the mammal brain, fills most of the skull. The mammal brain has quite different functions. When we come to the mammal brain we find for the first time a sense of community: love of women, of children, of the neighbor, the idea of brotherhood, care for the first time a sense of community: love of women for men, and men for women, love of children, of the neighbor, the idea of brotherhood, care for the community, or for the country. "There is no greater love than that of a man who will lay down his life for a friend". Evidently in the mammal brain there are two nodes of energy: sexual love and ferocity. (The reptile brain has no ferocity: it simply fights coldly for survival.) Women, it would seem, have strong mammal brains, and probably a correspondingly smaller energy channel to the reptile brain. They are more interested in love than war. "Make love, not war" means "move from the reptile brain to the mammal brain". Rock music is mammal music for the most part; long hair is mammal hair.

The Viking warrior who went "berserk" in battle may

have experienced the temporary capture of himself by the mammal brain. Eye witnesses reported that the face of the "berserk" appeared to change, and his strength increased fantastically — when he "woke up", he sometimes found he had killed twenty or thirty men. The facial expression is probably a union of the concerns of all three brains, so if one brain takes over, it is natural that the shape of the face would change.

What does the third brain, the "new brain", do? In late mammal times, the body evidently added a third brain. Brain researchers are not sure why — perhaps the addition is connected to the invention of tools, and the energy explosion that followed that. In any case, this third brain, which I shall call here the new brain, takes the form of an outer eighth inch of brain tissue laid over the surface of the mammal brain. It is known medically as the neo-cortex. Brain tissue of the neo-cortex is incredibly complicated, more so than the other brains, having millions of neurons per square inch. Curiously, the third brain seems to have been created for problems more complicated than those it is now being used for. Some neurologists speculate that an intelligent person today uses 1/100 of its power. Einstein may have been using 1/50 of it.

The only good speculations I have seen on the new brain, and what it is like, are in Charles Fair's book, *The Dying Self*, Wesleyan University Press. Fair suggests that what Freud meant by the "Id" was the reptile and mammal brain, and what the ancient Indian philosophers meant by the "self" was the new brain. His book is fascinating. He thinks that the new brain can grow and that its food is wild spiritual ideas. Christ said, "If a seed goes into the ground and dies, then it will grow". The reptile and mammal brains don't understand that sentence at all, both being naturalists, but the new brain understands it, and feels the excitement of it. The Greek mystery religions, and the Essene cult that Christ was a member of, were clear attempts to feed the new brain. The "mysteries" were the religion of the new brain. In Europe it was at its highest energy point about 1500, after knowing the ecstatic spiritual ideas of the Near East for 700 years. Since then, "secularization" means that the other two brains have increased their power. Nevertheless a man may still live if he wishes to more in his new brain than his neighbors do. Many of the parables of Christ, and the remarks of Buddha evidently involve instructions on how to transfer energy from the reptile brain to the mammal brain, and then to the new brain. A "saint" is someone who has managed to move away from the reptile and the mammal brains and is living primarily in the new brain. As the reptile brain power is symbolized by cold, and the mammal brain by warmth, the mark of the new brain is light. The gold light always around Buddha's head in statues is an attempt to suggest that he is living in his new brain. Some Tibetan meditators of the 13th century were able to read books in the dark by the light given off from their own bodies.

2.

If there is no central organization to the brain, it is clear that the three brains must be competing for all the available energy at any moment. The brains are like legislative committees — competing for government grants. A separate decision on apportionment is made in each head, although the whole tone of the society has weight on that decision. Whichever brain receives the most energy, that brain will determine the tone of that personality, regardless of his intelligence or "reasoning power". The United States, given the amount of fear it generates every day in its own citizens, as well as in the citizens of other nations, is a vast machine for throwing people into the reptile brain. The ecology workers, the poets, singers, meditators, rock musicians and many people in the younger generation in general, are trying desperately to reverse the contemporary energy-flow in the brain. Military appropriations cannot be reduced until the flow of energy in the brain, which has been moving for four or five centuries from the new brain to the reptile brain, is reversed. The reptile and the new brains are now trying to make themselves visible. The reptile brain has embodied itself in the outer world in the form of a tank which even moves like a reptile. Perhaps the computer is the new brain desperately throwing itself out into the world of objects so that we'll *see* it; the new brain's spirituality could not be projected, but at least its speed is apparent in the computer. The danger of course with the computer is that it may fall into the power of the reptile brain.

3.

We do not spend the whole day "inside" one brain, but we flip perhaps a thousand times a day from one brain to the other. Moreover we have been doing this flipping so long — since we were in the womb — that we no longer recognize the flips when they occur. If there is no central organization to the brain, and evidently there is not, it means that there is no "I". If your name is John there is no "John" inside you — there is no "I" at all. Oddly, that is the fundamental idea that Buddha had twenty-six hundred years ago. "I have news for you", he said, "there is no 'I' inside there. Therefore trying to find it is useless." The West misunderstands "meditation" or sitting because, being obsessed with unity and "identity", it assumes that the purpose of meditation is to achieve unity. On the contrary, the major value of sitting, particularly at the start, is to let the sitter experience the real chaos of the brain. Thoughts shoot in from all three brains in turn, and the sitter does not talk about, but *experiences* the lack of an 'I'. The lack of an 'I' is a central truth of Buddhism (Taoism expresses it by talking of the presence of a "flow"). Christianity somehow never arrived at this idea. At any rate, it never developed practical methods, like sitting, to allow each person to experience the truth himself. Institutional Christianity is in trouble because it depends on a pre-Buddhist model of the brain.

4.

Evidently spiritual growth for human beings depends on the ability to transfer energy. Energy that goes normally to the reptile brain can be transferred to the mammal brain, some of it at least; energy intended for the mammal brain can be transferred to the new brain.

The reptile brain thinks constantly of survival, of food, of security. When Christ says, "The lilies do not work, and yet they have better clothes than you do," he is urging his students not to care so much for themselves. If the student wills "not-caring", and that "not-caring" persists, the "not-caring" will eventually cause some transfer of energy away from the reptile brain. Voluntary poverty worked for St. Francis, and he had so little reptile brain paranoia the birds came down to sit on his shoulders.

If energy has been diverted from the reptile brain, the student, if he is lucky, can then transfer some of it to the mammal, and then to the new brain. Christ once advised his students, "If someone slaps you on the left cheek, point to the right cheek." The mammal brain loves to flare up and to strike back instantly. If you consistently refuse to allow the ferocity of the mammal brain to go forward into action, it will become discouraged, and some of its energy will be available for transfer. Since the mammal brain commits a lot of its energy to sexual love, some students at this point in the "road" become ascetic and celibate. They do so precisely in order to increase the speed of energy transfer. The women saints also, such as Anna of Foligno, experience this same turn in the road, which usually involves an abrupt abandonment of husband and children. Christ remarks in the Gospel of St. Thomas that some men are born eunuchs; and some men make themselves eunuchs in order to get to the Kingdom of the Spirit. However if a man is in the reptile brain at the time he begins his asceticism, then the result is a psychic disaster, as it has been for so many Catholic priests and monks.

The leap from the reptile to the new brain cannot be made directly; the student must go through the mammal brain. St. Theresa's spiritual prose shows much sexual imagery, perhaps because the mammal brain contributed its energy to the spiritual brain.

"Meditation" is a practical method for transferring energy from the reptile to the mammal brain, and then from the mammal to the new brain. It is slow, but a "wide" road, a road many can take, and many religious disciplines have adopted it. The orientals do not call it meditation, but "sitting". If the body sits in a room for an hour, quietly, doing nothing, the reptile brain becomes increasingly restless. It wants excitement, danger. In oriental meditation the body is sitting in the foetal position, and this further infuriates the reptile brain, since it is basically a mammalian position.

Of course if the sitter continues to sit, the mammal brain quickly becomes restless too. It wants excitement, confrontations, insults, sexual joy. It now starts to feed in spectacular erotic imagery, of the sort that St. Anthony's sittings were famous for. Yet if the sitter persists in doing nothing, eventually energy has nowhere to go but to the new brain.

Because Christianity has no "sitting", fewer men and women in Western culture than in oriental civilizations have been able to experience the ecstasy of the new brain. Thoreau managed to transfer a great deal of energy to the new brain without meditation, merely with the help of solitude. Solitude evidently helps the new brain. Thoreau of course willed his solitude and he was not in a reptile city, but in mammal or "mother" nature. Once more the truth holds that the road to the new brain passes through the mammal brain, through "the forest". This truth is embodied in ancient literature by the tradition of spiritual men meditating first in the forest and only after that in the desert. For the final part of the road, the desert is useful, because it contains almost no mammal images. Even in the desert, however, the saints preferred to live in caves — perhaps to remind the reptile brain of the path taken.

5.

To return to poetry, it is clear that poets, like anyone else, can be dominated by one of the three brains. Chaucer is a great poet of the mammal brain; clearly St. John of the Cross and Kabir are great poets of the new brain. The reptile brain seems to have no poet of its own, although occasionally that brain will influence poets. Robinson Jeffers is a man with an extremely powerful mammal brain, in whom, nevertheless, the reptile brain had a slight edge. His magnificent poems are not warm towards human beings. On the contrary, he has a curious love for the claw and the most ancient sea rocks. Every once in a while he says flatly that if all human beings died off, and a seal or two remained on earth, that would be all right with him.

Bach makes music of new brain emotions; Beethoven primarily out of mammal brain emotions. Blake is such an amazing poet because he talks of moving from one brain to another. His people in "the state of experience", after all, have been pulled back into the reptile brain.

> *The invisible worm*
> *That flies in the night,*
> *In the howling storm,*
> *Has found out thy bed*
> *Of crimson joy,*
> *And his dark secret love*
> *Does thy life destroy.*

When we are in a state of "innocence", Blake says we

are feeling some of the spiritual ecstasy of the new brain. The industrialists, as Blake saw clearly, are in a state of "experience", trapped by the reptile brain.

I think poetry ought to take account of these ideas. Some biological and neurological speculations are marvellous, and surely that speculation belongs in literary criticism as much as speculation about breath or images or meter. A person should try to feel what it is like to live in each of the three brains, and a poet could try to bring all three brains inside poems.

Robert Bly

FEDERICO GARCIA LORCA

CIUDAD SIN SUEÑO

(Nocturno del Brooklyn Bridge)

No duerme nadie por el cielo. Nadie, nadie.
No duerme nadie.
Las criaturas de la luna huelen y rondan sus cabañas.
Vendrán las iguanas vivas a morder a los hombres que no
      sueñan
y el que huye con el corazón roto encontrará por las
      esquinas
al increíble cocodrilo quieto bajo la tierna protesta
      de los astros.

    No duerme nadie por el mundo. Nadie, nadie.
No duerme nadie.
Hay un muerto en el cementerio más lejano
que se queja tres años
porque tiene un paisaje seco en la rodilla;
y el niño que enterraron esta mañana lloraba tanto
que hubo necesidad de llamar a los perros para que callase.

    No es sueño la vida. Alerta! Alerta! Alerta!
Nos caemos de las escaleras para comer la tierra húmeda
o subimos al filo de la nieve con el coro de las dalias
      muertas.
Pero no hay olvido, ni sueño:
carne viva. Los besos atan las bocas
en una maraña de venas recientes
y al que le duele su dolor le dolerá sin descanso
y al que teme la muerte la llevará sobre sus hombros.

    Un día
las caballos vivirán en las tabernas

CITY THAT DOES NOT SLEEP

(Nightsong of Brooklyn Bridge)

In the sky there is nobody asleep. Nobody, nobody.
Nobody is asleep.
The creatures of the moon sniff and prowl about their
    cabins.
The living iguanas will come to bite the men who do not
    dream,
and the man who rushes out with his spirit broken will
    meet on the street corner
the unbelievable alligator quiet beneath the tender protest
    of the stars.

Nobody is asleep on earth. Nobody, nobody.
Nobody is asleep.
In the graveyard far off there is a corpse
who has moaned for three years
because of a dry countryside in his knee;
and that boy they buried this morning cried so much
it was necessary to call out the dogs to keep him quiet.

Life is not a dream. Careful! Careful! Careful!
We fall down the stairs in order to eat the moist earth
or we climb to the knife edge of the snow with the voices
    of the dead dahlias.
But forgetfulness does not exist, dreams do not exist:
flesh exists. Kisses tie our mouths
in a thicket of new veins,
and whoever his pain pains will feel that pain forever
and whoever is afraid of death will carry it on his shoulders.

One day
the horses will live in the saloons

y las hormigas furiosas
atacarán los cielos amarillos que se refugian en los ojos
    de las vacas.

Otro día
veremos la resurrección de las mariposas disecadas
y aún andando por un paisaje de esponjas grises y barcos
    mudos
veremos brillar nuestro anillo y manar rosas de nuestra
    lengua.
¡Alerta! ¡Alerta! ¡Alerta!
A los que guardan todavía huellas de zarpa y aguacero,
a aquel muchacho que llora porque no sabe la invención
    del puente
o a aquel muerto que ya no tiene más que la cabeza y un
    zapato,
hay que llevarlos al muro donde iguanas y sierpes esperan,
donde espera la dentadura del oso,
donde espera la mano momificada del niño
y la piel del camello se eriza con un violento escalofrío
    azul.

No duerme nadie por el cielo. Nadie, nadie.
No duerme nadie.
¡Pero si alguien cierra los ojos,
azotadlo, hijos míos, azotadlo!
Haya un panorama de ojos abiertos
y amargas llagas encendidas.
No duerme nadie por el mundo. Nadie, nadie.
Ya lo he dicho.
No duerme nadie.
Pero si alguien tiene por la noche exceso de musgo en
    las sienes,
abrid los escotillones para que vea bajo la luna
las copas falsas, el veneno y la calavera de los teatros.

and the enraged ants
will throw themselves on the yellow skies that have taken
    refuge in the eyes of cows.

Another day
we will watch the preserved butterflies rise from the dead
and still walking through a country of gray sponges and
    silent boats
we will watch our ring flash and roses spring from our
    tongue.
Careful! Be careful! Be careful!
The men who still have marks of the claw and the
    thunderstorm,
and that boy who cries because he has never heard of the
    invention of the bridge,
or that dead man who only possesses now his head and
    a shoe,
we must carry them all to the wall where the iguanas and
    the snakes are waiting,
where the bear's teeth are waiting,
where the mummified hand of the boy is waiting,
and the hair of the camel stands on end with a violent blue
    shudder.

Nobody is sleeping in the sky. Nobody, nobody.
Nobody is sleeping.
If someone does close his eyes,
a whip, boys, a whip!
Let there be a landscape of open eyes
and bitter wounds on fire.
No one is sleeping in this world. No one, no one.
I have said it before.
No one is sleeping.
But if someone grows too much moss on his temples
    during the night,
open the stage trapdoors so he can see in the moonlight
the lying goblets, and the poison, and the skull of the
    theatres.

Translated by Robert Bly

SURREALISM, RILKE, AND LISTENING

IF WE go back and read some of the surrealist poems of Lorca, it's clear that Lorca is often leaping from one brain to the other. In "City That Does Not Sleep", Lorca pulls an image out of the memory bank of the mammal brain: "The creatures of the moon sniff and prowl about their cabins," and then immediately follows with an image from the memory bank of the reptile brain, "The living iguanas will come to bite the men who do not dream", and then an image from the memory bank of the new brain comes in: "The man who rushes out with his spirit broken . . ." He doesn't do it deliberately — that's simply how the brain works when it is confident and excited, and he sensed how the brain works better than any other poet so far.

Mere mechanical pulling of images out of memory stores will not produce leaping poetry; and that is possibly why so much mechanical surrealist poetry fails. Lorca's energy input to his new brain was immense, and he increased it by living and writing in a certain way. When the new brain is receiving energy from the other brains, then leaping poetry is possible. In other words, leaping poetry probably cannot be written without great spiritual energy.

Lorca's surrealist poems, the good ones, are models of the human brain. Shakespeare's sonnets are models too, but of the society in which he lived; as models of the human brain they fail. Poems of steady light always imply a unity in the brain that is not there. The reason we have surrealism in this century is because we are really interested in this century in how the brain works. The reason surrealism is weak in the United States is because the

North Americans are obsessed with unity and identity. The critical point of view represented by the *New York Review of Books* in America and *The Spectator* in England is hostile to surrealism, and longs for the old non-existent unity, which seems to them civilized and terribly elegant. Auden longed for that unity so much he first found it in Marxism, then in Christian doctrine, and at that point re-wrote his old Marxist poems to impose his second unity on them.

* * * * * *

Writers in American magazines talk very little about Rilke, yet surely he is the greatest spiritual poet of the twentieth century, and the greatest poet of the new brain. His earliest poems report the change in the Western psyche — the change that Jimenez described as the ship hitting something deep down. Poems in *A Book for the Hours of Prayer* (*Das Stundenbuch*) return to this sensation again and again. He notices the associative powers deepening. In a poem from *A Book for the Hours of Prayer*, he says:

> . . . . I want to describe myself
> like a painting that I saw
> a few feet off, and close up,
> like a word that I finally understood,
> like a pitcher I use every day,
> like the face of my mother,
> like a ship
> that took me safely
> through the wildest storm of all.

The last few lines have marvellous leaps. His poetry is always about change, paths, doors, roads opening. The story of Orpheus became important to him, because Orpheus was a man who kept his paths of association open. As Eliade noticed, Orpheus is an early shaman figure, who flies "from one world to the next". We know that Orpheus did keep his paths of association open because the animals understood everything he played, and he was always drawn with the animals around him, listening.

Toward the end of his life, Rilke began to describe the new powers — moving from one part of the brain to another, leaping quickly from conscious to unconscious — as if they were a new power in *listening*. It's an amazing idea. He imagines the road not as if it were a road over the sea but as if it were a thread of sound. To follow the sound . . . you must listen. That was why he thought the pictures of the animals listening to Orpheus were so marvellous — they emphasized listening.

Rilke then suggested Orpheus as a hero of the modern power of listening, though for years he had understood Orpheus also as an ancient hero of the great leap. Orpheus, in pursuit of "Eurydice", went down into the "dark world" and then returned to the "light world". This leap between two worlds became another theme of the *Sonnets to Orpheus*.

Robert Bly

SONNETS TO ORPHEUS

I

A tree rising. What a pure growing!
Orpheus is singing! A tree inside the ear!
Silence, silence. Yet new buildings,
signals, and changes went on in the silence.

Animals created by silence came forward from the clear
and relaxed forest where their lairs were,
and it turned out the reason they were so full of silence
was not cunning, and not terror,

it was listening. Growling, yelping, grunting now
seemed all nonsense to them. And where before
there was hardly a shed where this listening could go,

a rough shelter put up out of brushy longings,
with an entrance gate whose poles were wobbly,
you created a temple for them deep inside their ears.

III

A god can do it. But tell me, how can a man
follow his intricate road through the strings?
A man is split. And where two roads intersect
inside us, no one has built the Singer's Temple.

Writing poetry as we learn from you is not desiring,
not wanting something that can never be achieved.
To write poetry is to be alive. For a god that's easy.
When, however, are we really alive? And when does he

turn the earth and the stars so they face us?
Yes, you're young, and you love, and the voice
forces your mouth open — that's lovely, but learn

to forget that breaking into song. It doesn't last.
Real singing is a different movement of air.
Air moving around nothing. A breathing in a god. A wind.

VI

Is he from our world? No, his deep nature
grows out of both of the kingdoms.
He can bend down the branches of the willow best
who has experienced the roots of the willow.

When you go to bed, do not leave bread
behind on the table, or milk; it will entice the dead.
But Orpheus, a shaman, infuses their spirits
into everything that can be seen

beneath the quietness of the closed eyes;
and the magic meaning of rue and smokeherb
is as clear to him as the sharpest logic.

Nothing can blur the real image for him;
whether drawn from tombs or from our houses
he praises the ring, the clasp, and the water jar!

IX

Only the man who has raised his strings
among the dark ghosts also
can sense it and give
the everlasting praise.

Only he who has eaten poppy
with the dead, from their poppy,
will never lose even
his most delicate sound.

Even though images in the pool
seem so blurry:
grasp the main thing.

Only in the double kingdom, there
alone, do voices become
undying and tender.

Translated by Robert Bly

HOME GROWN POEMS

VOZNESENSKY SAID a few years ago, "Rhyme has become boring. In poetry the future lies with the ability to associate." And Russian poetry has a lot of leaping. So has South American poetry, and "primitive" poetry.

In leaping, we are the dolts. The whole mood of our culture suggests that if a man writes of war or of vomit, he need have nothing to do with the spirit; if a man writes of the spirit, he is excused from any visits to the mammal world. So how can there be leaping? Our living poets tend to be specialists in one world. And the magazines go on talking about the exclusively literary, where to break lines or make reputations or the title of Mark Strand's new book or who is teaching, now, at the University of Iowa's arthritic Workshop.

But despite all that, we do have leapers. And here is a sampling, including old hands and new hands. There are many more poets, both English and American, who belong here, but even these few suggest the varieties of mood possible.

GREG ORR

THIS LIFE LIKE NO OTHER...

> This life like no other.
> The bread rising in the ditches.
> The bellies of women swelling
> with air.
> Walking alone under the dark pines,
> a blue leather bridle in my hand.

BILL KNOTT

PROSEPOEM TO HART CRANE

India and China, please help, there is a famine here, an America-famine, there's no longer enough America to feed Whitman or Poe, and I'm getting very thin. Oh dropping bombs upon what no longer exists! Glances traveling through life and death, meeting only at the moment of and the moment of. Touching. Hart, heart of America, are we falling through you only to enter an extinct language? No, we'll breed no more sun. Don't walk in conception. His birthplace says goodbye; leaves us; is yet to be. Whooping-cranes are already extinct in our pre-coital play.

from THE CAR CRASH POEM

III

Raw pine walls, ice-white windows
three weeks now, snowy flatness
foot-thick down valley meadows,
wind roar in bare ash arms, oak branch
tendrils icy gleaming, yellow
stain of morning water in front
door's snow — I walk out on crutches
to see white moonglow make snow blue
— three men just rode a space ship
round the moon last week — gnashing
their teeth in Biafra & Palestine,
Assassins & Astronauts travelling from
Athens to the sea of Venus Creatrix —
Lover's quarrels magnified decades to mad
violence, half naked farm boys stand
with axes at the kitchen table,
trembling guilty, slicing egg
grapefruit breasts on breakfast oilcloth.
Growing old, growing old, forget the words,
mind jumps to the grave, forget words,
Love's an old word, forget words,
Peter with shave-head beardface
mutters & screams to himself at midnight.
A new year, no party tonite, forget
old loves, old words, old feelings.
Snow everywhere around the house,
I turned off the gas-light & came upstairs
alone to read, remembering pictures of dead
moon-side, my hip broken, the cat sick,
earhead filled with my own strong music,

in a houseful of men, sleep in underwear.
Neal almost a year turned to ash, angel
in his own midnight without a phonecall,
Jack drunk in my mind or his Florida.
Forget old friends, old words, old loves,
old bodies. Bhaktivedanta advises Christ.
The body lies in bed in '69 alone,
a gnostic book fills the lap, Aeons
revolve round the household, Rimbaud
age 16 Adolescent sneers tight lipt
green eyed oval in old time gravure
— 1869 his velvet tie askew, hair
mussed & ruffled by policemen's rape.

                              1:30 AM Jan 1, 1969

CONJUGAL

A man is bending his wife.
He is bending her around something that she has bent
herself around.
She is around it, bent as he has bent her.

He is convincing her.
It is all so private between them.

He bends her around the bedpost.
No, he is bending her around the tripod of his camera.
It is as if he teaches her to swim
as if he teaches acrobatics
as if he could form her into something wet
that he delivers out of one life into another.

And it is such a private thing the thing they do.

He is forming her into the wallpaper
he is smoothing her down into the flowers there
and he is finding her nipples there
and he is kissing her pubis.

He is climbing into the wallpaper among the flowers
his buttocks moves in and out of the wall.

REPOSE OF RIVERS

The willows carried a slow sound,
A sarabande the wind mowed on the mead.
I could never remember
That seething, steady leveling of the marshes
Till age had brought me to the sea.

Flags, weeds. And remembrance of steep alcoves
Where cypresses shared the noon's
Tyranny; they drew me into hades almost.
And mammoth turtles climbing sulphur dreams
Yielded, while sun-silt rippled them
Asunder . . .

How much I would have bartered! the black gorge
And all the singular nestings in the hills
Where beavers learn stitch and tooth.
The pond I entered once and quickly fled —
I remember now its singing willow rim.

And finally, in that memory all things nurse;
After the city that I finally passed
With scalding unguents spread and smoking darts
The monsoon cut across the delta
At gulf gates . . . There, beyond the dykes

I heard wind flaking sapphire, like this summer,
And willows could not hold more steady sound.

WINTER SCENE

So earth's inclined toward the one invisible,
The prince of space, and yet he was disproved,
But this is her nuptial night, a cruel season
As limbless lizards coil together in love

And her whiteness veils over the dog-faced owl,
Whiteness veils over the frozen streams, the moon,
And the deer islanded without family,
Nuzzling cold tulips. Whiteness veils over the sea,

And the heart of the snail is beating slow.
But as an early bride, with heaven's rose
She is adorned, she is wound in seven veils
Even as a bride going forth to the bridegroom,

And her whiteness veils over the scarred fields.
She is celebrant for the failure of a theory,
And the white ptarmigan treads in the snow
                    among the low hills.

from SLEEPERS JOINING HANDS

There are fears that come up from underneath,
bushes moving where there is no wind,
Christ bound on a burning wheel,
Do not be afraid.
The sun hidden by great insects,
a snake curled around the flower jar on the grave,
so many die mad, knocking over chairs,
the battle we can lose, maybe
have already lost,
numbness, nothingness, paralysis!
The hawks will dive on us, the mother-hawk will come,
we will be taken,
eaten in a valley,
bones scattered, hair thrown into the wind!
In that age no one can save himself,
        the Saviour himself caught
        in a magnetic field,
"struggling against his swaddling bands."

There are fears coming up from underneath,
pulling us down,
the ecstatic orifices closed to the blue stormlight,
Antares and the Orphic nests swirled in the surd rivers,
the outer eight-inch of the brain giving off smoke,
        like mist boiling off hailclouds,
I am afraid.
The insubstantial bodies stretched out ten miles long in
        the sixth dimension,
the death birds flying along the corridors we make for
        them with our own bodies after death,
ships rising and falling, no way out.

JOHN WIENERS

TWO YEARS LATER

The hollow eyes of shock remain
Electric sockets burnt out in the
     skull.

The beauty of men never disappears
But drives a blue car through the
                  stars.

CRAZY DOG EVENTS

CROW INDIAN

1. Act like a crazy dog. Wear sashes & other fine clothes, carry a rattle, & dance along the roads singing crazy dog songs after everybody else has gone to bed.

2. Talk crosswise: say the opposite of what you mean & make others say the opposite of what they mean in return.

3. Fight like a fool by rushing up to an enemy & offering to be killed. Dig a hole near an enemy, & when the enemy surrounds it, leap out at them & drive them back.

4. Paint yourself white, mount a white horse, cover its eyes & make it jump down a steep & rocky bank, until both of you are crushed.

arranged: 12-11-70

RAYMOND ZDONEK

THREADS IX

The way the streetlamp casts my shadow off
My back porch; I keep expecting
Someone to be crossing
The deep sleeping grass.

GREG ORR

SILENCE

The way the word sinks into the deep snow of the page.

The dead deer lying in the clearing,
its head and antlers transparent.
The black seed in its brain
parachuting toward earth.

THE WAY WEST   UNDERGROUND

Split-cedar
smoked salmon
cloudy days of Oregon,
the thick fir forests.
     Black Bear heads uphill in
     Plumas county,
     round bottom scuttling through willows —

The Bear wife moves up the coast.
     blackberry brambles
        ramble
     in the burns —

And around the curve of islands
foggy volcanoes
on to North Japan. the bears
& fish-spear of the Ainu,
Gilyak,
mushroom-vision healer,
single flat drum
     from long before China —

Women with drums who fly
     over Tibet.
following forests west, and
rolling, following grassland,
tracking bears and mushrooms,
eating berries all the way.
in Finland finally took a bath

Like redwood sweatlodge on the Klamath —
all the Finns in moccasins and
pointy hats with dots of white —
netting, trapping,
bathing,
singing holding hands, the while
      see-sawing on a bench, a look of love —
Karhu — Bjorn — Braun — Bear

      lightning rainbow great cloud tree,
         dialogs of birds

Europa. "The West"
the bears are gone
      except Brunhilde?

or elder wilder goddesses reborn — will race
      the streets of France and Spain
         with automatic guns —

      in Spain,
Bears and Bison
Red hands with missing fingers,
Red mushroom labyrinths;
Lightning-bolt mazes,

Underground.

from THE NEWCASTLE POEM

Dissolve, dissolve
reduce to cotton wool
& still dissolve

reduce to white sea foam
& still dissolve

dissolve to fishes in the sea
& still dissolve

dissolve into the eggs beneath the leaf
& still dissolve

dissolve to fibres in the roots
& still dissolve

dissolve into a fishes eye
& still dissolve

dissolve into a sea gulls beak
and still dissolve

dissolve into its chalky crap
and still dissolve

dissolve into the salt upon the sea
and still dissolve

dissolve into a spot of blood
& still dissolve

dissolve into a kiss
& still dissolve

dissolve into a tongue
and still dissolve

dissolve into a lick
& still dissolve

dissolve into a mirrow's eye
& still dissolve

dissolve into your own desire
& still dissolve

dissolve into her warmest fur
& still dissolve

dissolve into the air
& still dissolve

dissolve into her breast of milk
& still dissolve

dissolve into your sucking lips
& still dissolve

the milk burns in your throat

the flame is yours
you are the flame

there is no name
you are the name

The rivers voice is many flamed

Acknowledgments

We are grateful to the following poets, translators, publishing houses, and copyright holders for permission to include texts in this volume:

CESAR VALLEJO—"Poema para ser leído y cantado" ("Poem to Be Read and Sung"); "Tengo un miedo terrible . . ." ("I Have a Terrible Fear . . ."); "¡Y si después de tantas palabras . . ." ("And What if After So Many Words . . ."); "¿Y bien? Te sana el metaloide palido . . ." ("And So? The Pale Metalloid Heals You . . ."). In Spanish, and in English translation by Robert Bly, printed with the kind permission of Mme. Georgette de Vallejo.

PABLO NERUDA—"The Ruined Street" in a translation by Robert Bly. Published by permission of New Directions, publishers of Pablo Neruda, *Residence on Earth*, translated by Donald D. Walsh. Copyright © 1973 by New Directions Publishing Corporation.

BLAS DE OTERO—"Una especie de" ("Something Like A") and "Loyalty," in translation by Hardie St. Martin, with his permission. Spanish versions printed with the kind permission of Blas de Otero.

GUNNAR EKELÖF—"Monologue with Its Wife," Albert Bonniers Förlag, Publishers, Stockholm, Sweden. Copyright © 1955 by Bonniers.

TOMAS TRANSTRÖMER—"Out in the Open," in translation by Robert Bly, printed with the kind permission of Tomas Tranströmer.

RAINER MARIA RILKE—Sonnets I, III, VI, IX of *Sonnets to Orpheus*, in translation by Robert Bly, and in German, printed with permission of W.W. Norton & Co., New York.

GREGORY ORR—"Poem" ("This Life Like . . .") and "Silence," from *Burning the Empty Nests*, by Gregory Orr. Copyright © 1973 by Gregory Orr. By permission of Harper & Row, Publishers, Inc.

BILL KNOTT—"Prosepoem to Hart Crane," copyright 1972 by Bill Knott. Printed with the kind permission of the author.

ALLEN GINSBERG—Selection III from "The Car Crash Poem," from *The Fall of America*. Copyright © 1972 by Allen Ginsberg. Reprinted by permission of City Lights Books.

RUSSELL EDSON—"Conjugal," from *The Childhood of an Equestrian*, by Russell Edson. By permission of Harper & Row, Publishers, Inc.

HART CRANE—"Repose of Rivers," from *The Collected Poems and Selected Letters and Prose of Hart Crane*, by Hart Crane. Permission of Liveright Publishing, New York. Copyright © 1933, 1958, 1966 by Liveright Publishing Corporation.